HEAVEN

by
William MacDonald

EVERYDAY PUBLICATIONS INC.
310 KILLALY ST. W.
PORT COLBORNE, ON, CANADA L3K 6A6

Copyright © 1996, William MacDonald
ISBN 978-0-88873-714-94 **Revision - 1999**

This is an enlarged edition of the book
HEAVEN: Himself, Home, Holiness, Happiness, Hallelujah,
published by Everyday Publications.

Unless otherwise noted, all Bible references
are quoted from the New King James Version,
© 1979, 1980, 1982,
Thomas Nelson Inc., Publishers.

Abbreviations

KJV	King James Version
NKJV	New King James Version
JND	J.N. Darby's New Translation
NASB	New American Standard Bible
NIV	New International Version
RSV	Revised Standard Version

Cover design by Tom Miller

Printed in Canada

Table of Contents

What Will Heaven Be Like?

Most people think that we can't know much about heaven. Conventional wisdom limits us to a short list of negatives: no sun, no moon, no night, no sea, no sickness, no sorrow, no suffering, no tears, no death. Oh yes, it will admittedly be *outstanding*, but beyond that we don't know much.

It's true that we don't know all we might want to know in order to satisfy our curiosity about our heavenly home. But it's surprising how much we can know about the place the Savior has gone to prepare. If we just use the straight facts of Scripture, the clues that are strongly implied, and a little sanctified imagination, we can form an amazingly detailed picture of an amazingly delightful place.

1
THE WAY TO GOD

The Bible speaks of two main highways on the landscape of life. One is a broad road, the other narrow. The first is not broad because it is smoother, more reasonable, or more certain. Rather, it's the more heavily traveled. The second is narrow because not many choose it, not because it's difficult, uncertain, or impassable.

The broad road represents the popular doctrine of "salvation by works." Those who travel on it seek to earn or deserve eternal life. Most people think that this is the right way (Prov. 14:12). The narrow way offers salvation as a free gift to those who repent of their sins and receive the Lord Jesus Christ by faith. They acknowledge that they don't deserve salvation, but, on the contrary, deserve the opposite.

The broad road leads to destruction (Prov. 16:25). The destination of those on the narrow road is heaven.

The Savior equates Himself with the narrow way, saying, "I am the way, the truth and the life. No one comes to the Father except through Me" (John 14:6).

In order to get on the broad road, a person doesn't have to do anything; we are all on it from birth. To get on the narrow way we must:

a.– leave the broad road by renouncing all efforts to save ourselves by good works or good character;

b.– repent of our sins;

c.– believe that the Savior died on the cross as our Substitute, paying the penalty for all our sins;

d.–then, by a definite act of faith, receive Jesus Christ as our Lord and Savior, depending on Him alone as our right to go to heaven.

As soon as any of us does that, we are on the narrow road that leads to life. We are saved from hell. We are converted to God. We are made fit for "the inheritance of the saints in light" (Col. 1:12 KJV). We are as sure of heaven as if we were already there.

2

IN THE HEAVENLIES

Surprise! As soon as a person is born again, there is a sense in which he or she is already in heaven. Paul wrote to the believers in Ephesus that they were "blessed with every spiritual blessing in the heavenly places in Christ" (Eph. 1:3). Further, they were sitting together "in the heavenly places in Christ Jesus" (Eph. 2:6).

These truths are difficult for many of us to understand. They seem rather ethereal, mystical, even unreal.

It is clear that the heavenly places are the same as heaven itself because in Ephesians 1:20 the apostle says that the saints are where Christ is, seated at the right hand of God. Obviously He is in heaven at the present time.

In what sense then are Christians now in heaven. Well, this is our position in Christ. It is how God sees us. The truth that we are already in the heavenly places is something we must appropriate by faith. It is not something we feel but something we know, because God has said it.

What practical effect should this have on our lives? It means we should see things from His vantage point. As we look at a world that lies under the control of the evil one, we will want to share the gospel with those who are perishing. We will not allow ourselves to become entangled in the affairs of this life (2 Tim. 2:4). We will set our affections on things above, not on things on the earth (Col. 3:2). In general we will try to conduct ourselves as citizens of heaven (Phil. 3:20a).

Perhaps you've heard of people who lived in heaven long before they ever got there. If so, it's because they appropriated the truth that "positionally" they were seated together in the heavenly places in Christ Jesus. Then they made that truth practical in their lives.

I often think of Corrie Ten Boom and her sister Betsy, who suffered untold humiliation and pain in a Nazi concentration camp. One day Betsy said to Corrie, "When we get out of here, we have to do something for these people." Corrie naturally assumed that she was talking about their fellow-inmates in the camp. But no! Betsy was referring to the brutish guards and other workers bent on making life as miserable as possible. Corrie later wrote, "And I wondered, not for the first time, what sort of person she was, this sister of mine . . . what kind of road she followed while I trudged beside her on the all-too-solid earth." Betsy was living in the heavenlies although her feet were planted on the ground of a death-camp. And Corrie was, too, in spite of her protests to the contrary.

Lila Trotman is another example of an other-worldly lifestyle. One day she looked out over Schroon Lake where her husband, in the distance, was struggling in the water to save another person. When someone came to her with the news that her husband Dawson had drowned, her immediate reaction was to quote 1 Samuel 3:18, "It is the Lord. Let Him do what seems good to Him."

Another illustration of a heavenly walk took place during World War II. An eager young convert rushed up to a godly believer and enthusiastically reported, "Our bombers were over the enemy again last night." The older man commented, "I didn't know that the church of God had bombers." His citizenship was in another kingdom.

Vernon Schlief tells of a couple who attended a chapel that was adjacent to their farm. One Lord's Day, while they were remembering the Lord and worshiping Him, the wife looked out the window and saw that their barn was on fire. She leaned over and whispered to her husband, "Dear, our barn is on fire." He lifted his head and answered, "Hush, dear, the Lord is in this place." Is such a response extreme and impractical? Not really. He was just appropriating the truth that where two or three are gathered in the Lord's name, He is there in the midst (Matt. 18:20). Of what importance is a barn when we are in the presence of the Lord? And even if the man had left to fight the fire, what good would a garden hose do when a barn filled with hay was aflame?

3

DEATH OR RAPTURE

Although it is true that there is only one way of salvation, one way by which we are made fit for heaven, there are two ways by which we may be transported there. One is death, the other is the rapture.

Death

What happens when a person dies? The body goes to the grave while the spirit and soul go to heaven or hades, depending on the person's spiritual condition. One of the great illusions of life is that the body is the person. The fact is that the body is only the house or tent in which the person dwells.

We can live without the body. Neither God the Father nor the Holy Spirit has a body. Before He came to Bethlehem, the Lord Jesus did not have a body. In the story of the rich man and Lazarus, the rich man died and his body was buried. Yet he was conscious, could talk, could see, could suffer thirst and torment, could remember, and could be concerned about the eternal welfare of his five brothers (Luke 16:28).

A believer can exist in three conditions: in the body, disembodied, and in a glorified body. In 2 Corinthians 5, the apostle Paul described these three conditions as (1) in this tent, v.4, (2) unclothed or naked, vv.3,5, and (3) clothed upon, that is, with the glorified body, vv.3-4. The first state is good, the second is better, and the third is best of all.

For believers, death is the messenger of God that brings us to heaven. The moment we die we are instantly in the Father's house, consciously enjoying the Lord Jesus and all the glories of heaven. We don't need a body any more than Christ needed one before His incarnation, or during those three days and three nights when His body was in Joseph's tomb and He was in heaven with the thief who died believing.

Several times the New Testament speaks of a dead believer as sleeping (1 Cor. 11:30; 15:51; 1 Thess. 4:14). That description, however, refers only to the body. We might hear people in a funeral home say, "He looks just as if he were sleeping." It's the language of human appearance. The spirit and soul, that is, the person himself, does not sleep. As we have seen, if he is a Christian, he now is living with Christ. But it looks as if he is sleeping.

There is no intermediate body between death and the rapture. Some people cite 2 Corinthians 5:1 as proof that there is one: "For we know that if our earthly house, this tent, is destroyed, we have a building from God, a house not made with hands, eternal in the heavens." Those words can refer only to the final, glorified body because it is "eternal in the heavens." That would not be true of an intermediate body. But it is true of the glorified body which we receive at the time of the rapture. It is described as "not made with hands." This expression is explained in Hebrews 9:11 as meaning "not of this creation." In other words, the glorified body is specially designed for heaven, not for this earth.

Should a person fear death? It depends. If he is an unbeliever, there is every reason to fear. For him, death has a sting, namely, sins unconfessed and unforgiven. He goes to meet God and hear his sentence–eternal doom.

Believers need not fear death though we may not relish the thought of the suffering that may precede it. We can all identify with the old saint who said, "I don't mind the Lord's taking down my tent, but I just hope he'll take it down gently." Even in the process of dying, however, we have the promise that the Lord will never leave nor forsake us. On a more mundane note, modern medicine has sedatives so powerful that it is no longer necessary to endure excruciating pain.

The widow of a martyr in Ecuador wrote this poem to be read at her husband's memorial service:

The Other Side

This isn't death—it's glory;
It isn't dark—it's light;
It isn't stumbling, groping, or even faith—it's sight;
It isn't grief—it's having my last tear wiped away;
It is sunrise—the morning of my eternal day;
This isn't praying—it's speaking face to face,
And it's glimpsing all the wonders of His grace;
This is the end of all pleading for strength to bear my pain;
Not even pain's dark memory will ever live again;
How did I bear the earth life before I came up higher?
Before my soul was granted its every deep desire?
Before I knew this rapture of meeting face to face

With that one who sought me, saved me,
And kept me by His grace?"

This isn't death—it's glory![1]

As for death itself, it is a friend, not an enemy. The apostle reminds us that "to die is gain" (Phil. 1:21). It means to "depart and be with Christ, which is far better" (Phil. 1:23). So "we are confident, yes, well pleased rather to be absent from the body and to be present with the Lord" (2 Cor. 5:8). The more we take possession of this truth, the more we will look forward to entering the palace and seeing the King in His beauty. That is why John Wesley could say, "Our people [that is, Christian believers] die well."

Light after darkness, gain after loss;
Strength after weakness, crown after cross.
Sweet after bitter, hope after fears;
Home after wandering, praise after tears.
Sheaves after sowing, sun after rain;
Sight after mystery, peace after pain.
Joy after sorrow, calm after blast;
Rest after weariness, sweet rest at last.
Near after distant, gleam after gloom;
Love after loneliness, life after tomb.
After long agony, rapture of bliss;
Right was the pathway leading to this.
Now comes the weeping, then the glad reaping;
Now comes the labor hard, then the reward.

— Anonymous

What about the sorrow of leaving loved ones behind? This sorrow is real. But if they are God's children, the separation is only for a little while. We don't say "goodbye" but "until we meet again." If they are still in their sins, we can pray that our death may be the means of bringing them to the Lord. We can commit them to Him and to the convicting, converting power of the Holy Spirit.

If we are going to be realistic, we should face the fact that we may be called to go to heaven by way of death. But there is another possibility, the rapture.

The Rapture

Around 52 AD the apostle Paul revealed a truth that had never been known before. Speaking by divine inspiration, he announced that not everyone would die. Some would be taken home to heaven without passing through the valley of the shadow. He said that the bodies of those who had died in faith would be raised, glorified, and instantly vanish to heaven (1 Cor. 15:51-55). This unprecedented event is known as the rapture, from a Latin word meaning to carry or catch away.

Here are some of the essential features of the rapture:

The time is unknown, which means that it could happen at any moment. There will be no celestial signs of its nearness.

The Lord Jesus Himself will descend from heaven with a shout, the voice of the archangel, and the trumpet of God (1 Thess. 4:16a). Notice the emphasis on the word

Himself. This is not a mission He will entrust to an angel. It will be a personal appearance of the Lord Himself. His shout summons all believers, living or dead, to the great meeting in the air. Since the archangel is primarily concerned with the people of Israel (Daniel 12:1; Jude 9), the mention of his voice may be a suggestion that the Old Testament saints are raised at this time. The trumpet of God here is not to be confused with the seventh trumpet in Revelation 11. There it is a trumpet of judgment, here of blessing.

The bodies of those who have died believing in Christ will rise from the graves (1 Thess. 4:16b). It should be clear that this is not a general resurrection "at the end of the world," as some believe. Only the bodies of those who have died in faith will be raised at this time. Their souls and spirits, having come back from heaven with Christ, will be reunited with their new kind of bodies, just like the Savior's (1 Cor. 15:52-54; Phil. 3:21).

Living saints will be caught up with them to meet Christ in the air and to go with Him to the Father's house (1 Thess. 4:17). "So the ransomed of the Lord shall return, and come to Zion with singing, with everlasting joy on their heads. They shall obtain joy and gladness; sorrow and sighing shall flee away" (Isa. 51:11).

It all takes place in a moment, in the twinkling of an eye (1 Cor. 15:52a). Perhaps it is not exaggerating to say that the whole glorious event will happen in a nanosecond, that is, a billionth part of a second. Believers will vanish from sight instantly. That being so, there is no possibility that those who are left behind will see it happening. No wonder it has been called a secret rapture.

The rapture is the blessed hope of believers. If given a choice, we all would rather go to heaven without dying, even if the net result is the same. H. L. Turner expressed the average Christian's desire:

Oh joy! Oh delight, should we go without dying,
No sickness, no sadness, no dread, and no crying,
Caught up thro' the clouds with our Lord into glory,
When Jesus receives His own.

Sometimes Paul spoke of himself as one who would be alive when the Lord returns: " . . . we who are alive and remain" (1 Thess. 4:17). At other times he expected to die: "For I am already being poured out as a drink offering, and the time of my departure is at hand" (2 Tim. 4:6). That should be the attitude of every Christian. We should be ready for either event.

4

THE KING THERE IN HIS BEAUTY

The central fact of heaven is that the Lord Jesus will be there. He is there in surpassing splendor and indescribable beauty, His countenance shining as the sun in its strength. He is there as the Chief among ten thousand, the altogether lovely One. Every physical beauty and moral excellence are combined in Him.

> *Heaven for me, heaven for me;*
> *Jesus will be what makes it heaven for me.*
> *All its beauties and wonders I'm longing to see;*
> *But Jesus will be what makes it heaven for me.*
> — Lanny Wolfe

The vision of the exalted Lord is so supernal that writers have traditionally abandoned prose for poetry and music in an effort to capture the glory of His Person. Next to Calvary itself, perhaps the most frequent theme of Christian poetry is the face-to-face meeting with our Lord in heaven. But even poetry falters and words bend under the weight of superlatives.

Many of us are familiar with these lines by Carrie E. Breck:

> *Face to face with Christ my Savior,*
> *Face to face, what will it be,*
> *When with rapture I behold Him,*
> *Jesus Christ who died for me.*

Not so familiar is this exquisite verse by an unknown author:

> *Not merely one glimpse but forever,*
> *At home with Him ever to be,*
> *At home in the glory celestial*
> *Where shimmers the crystal sea.*
> *But there, even there in that glory*
> *Will anything ever efface*
> *That rapturous moment of moments,*
> *My first, first look at His face?*

Fanny Crosby, the blind poet, loved to dwell on the time when her eyes would be opened to see the Lord in His splendor and glory:

> *Oh, the soul-thrilling rapture when I see His*
> *blessed face,*
> *And the luster of His kindly beaming eye;*
> *How my full heart will praise Him for the*
> *mercy, love, and grace,*
> *That prepare for me a mansion in the sky.*

Another writer exults:

Glorious day when we stand in His presence,
When all our heartaches and sorrows are past,
When earth's best beauties fade as a flower,
We shall see Jesus at last!

— A.H.D.

The Lord Jesus is in heaven in a real physical body, one that He himself described as consisting of flesh and bones (Luke 24:39-40). (He made no mention of blood, since that was shed at Calvary.) He showed the disciples His hands and His side (John 20:20) and invited doubting Thomas to touch His hands and put his finger into His side (John 20:27). It is the same body in which He rose from the grave. In some ways it is similar to the one He received at birth; it has physical resemblance. The risen Lord could still eat food. On one occasion He ate broiled fish and some honeycomb (Luke 24:41-43, see also Luke 24:30; John 21:12). He could handle objects and could speak, see, and hear. He walked with two forlorn disciples on the road to Emmaus (Luke 24:15).

In other ways His body was and is different. It was not limited by time, space, or matter. He could enter a room when the doors and windows were shut (John 20:26). He could move about without apparent physical exertion (Luke 24:36), appearing and disappearing at will (Luke 24:31). It is a body that is suited to life in heaven as well as earth. But the most striking difference is that it still bears the marks of Calvary. After His resurrection He showed Thomas and the other disciples those wounds of divine love (Luke 24:40; John 20:20,27). John later described Him in glory as a lamb, as it were, freshly slain (Rev. 5:6). Think of it. The only marks of suffering and death in heaven serve as eternal reminders of the cost of our redemption. Spurgeon exults,[2]

> Oh, to see the feet that were nailed, and to touch the hands that were pierced, and to look upon the head that wore the thorns, and to bow before Him who is ineffable love, unspeakable condescension, infinite tenderness. Oh, to bow before Him, and to kiss that blessed face!

> *Thy wounds, Thy wounds, Lord Jesus,*
> *Those deep, deep wounds will tell*
> *The sacrifice that frees us*
> *From self, and death, and hell.*
> — C. A. H.

Most of us go through life looking for a perfect person. There is that deep desire within us to find a flawless individual. Sometimes we are privileged to meet people who have unusually splendid characteristics; they are refined, gracious, kind, and generous. But the more we get acquainted, the more we realize that they have some weakness, some vestige of the Fall, just like ourselves. Our hopes are dashed. But when we see the Savior, we will see the One who fulfills all our longings for excellence. He is the Perfect Son of God.

It is true here on earth, as Lew Wallace said, that beauty is in the eye of the beholder. A man who is handsome to one onlooker may not be to another. Likewise not everyone agrees on what makes a woman beautiful. But when we gaze on the Lord Jesus in heaven, there will be no disagreement. Everyone will agree that "He is altogether lovely, the Fairest of the fair." He will combine every beauty that we saw in isolation in this world.

When we see Him, we will have to exclaim, "The half had not been told."

> *Millions of years my wondering eyes*
> *Shall o'er Thy beauties rove.*
> *And endless ages I'll adore*
> *The glories of Thy love.*

—Anonymous

Is it likely that when we see the Lord we will marvel that we did not love Him more, serve Him better, and live for Him more completely when we were here on earth? One hymn writer thought so:

> *By and by when I look on His face,*
> *Beautiful face, thorn-shadowed face.*
> *By and by when I look on His face,*
> *I'll wish I had given Him more.*
> *More, so much more;*
> *More of my life than I e'er gave before.*
> *By and by when I look on His face,*
> *I'll wish I had given Him more.*
>
> *By and by when He holds out His hands,*
> *Welcoming hands, nail-pierced hands.*
> *By and by when He holds out His hands,*
> *I'll wish I had given Him more.*
> *More, so much more;*
> *More of my heart than I e'er gave before.*
> *By and by when He holds out His hands,*
> *I'll wish I had given Him more.*

By and by when I kneel at His feet,
Beautiful feet, nail-riven feet.
By and by when I kneel at His feet,
I'll wish I had given Him more.
More, so much more;
More of my heart than I e'er gave before.
By and by when I kneel at His feet,
I'll wish I had given Him more.

In one of his magnificent hymns, Robert Murray McCheyne (1813-1843) looked forward to the time when we will realize how much we owe the King of all kings.

When I stand before the throne,
Dressed in beauty not my own;
When I see Thee as Thou art,
Love Thee with unsinning heart;
Then, Lord, shall I fully know–
Not till then–how much I owe.

With all due respect to McCheyne, I think that even eternity will not exhaust the dimensions of our debt. It is infinite.

It is impossible to think of heaven without thinking of the Lord Jesus. The hymn writer, John Peterson, once submitted a script about our eternal home to a publisher for possible acceptance. The lyrics came back with the suggestion: "Take out the name *Jesus*, and enlarge a little more on heaven." Peterson found that utterly unthinkable and gave the hymn to another publisher.

Another writer anticipated heaven with these words:

To gaze on that face which was marred for me,
To touch those hands that were nailed to the tree,
To be pressed so close to that wounded side,
Where blood gushed out when it opened wide,
To kiss those feet that once trod the sea,
Will be joy supreme through eternity.

To bow at that throne of ineffable light,
Encircled with glory and rainbow bright,
To hear that voice that once calmed the sea,
Bade the winds be still, and demons flee;
To hear Him speak, and speak to me,
Will be joy supreme through eternity.

To serve in the home of endless delight,
With no need of candle for there is no night,
To sing with the choir of the heavenly host,
All glory to Father, Son, Holy Ghost;
Oh, wonder of wonders, all this for me,
Will be joy supreme through eternity.

– Anonymous

5

Other Residents

But the Savior will not be alone. With Him in glory will be an innumerable company of unfallen angels, ministering spirits who have served the heirs of salvation (Heb. 1:14; 12:22). Every believer has had one or more guardian angels. It is reasonable to believe that we will meet them and hear how they were responsible for our narrow escapes, miraculous deliverances, cliff-hanging experiences, and protection from unknown dangers. Though exalted in position, these celestial beings will be only spectators to the joy of our salvation. They will never be able to join in the songs of the redeemed.

The Church will be there: the general assembly and Church of the firstborn ones who are registered in heaven. We will mingle with all the ransomed throng from Pentecost to the rapture. There will be some from every nation, tribe, people, and tongue. The apostles and the martyrs will be there, as well as God's hidden ones who never made the headlines but served Him faithfully. We will fellowship with Matthew, Mark, Luke, and John, and with Luther, Calvin, Spurgeon, and Müller.

Can we really be sure that there will be recognition in heaven? First, it is certain we will not know *less* than what we do now. Second, Paul expected to recognize the Thessalonians on the other side; they would be his joy and crown of rejoicing (1 Thess. 2:19-20). He anticipated mutual joy between the Corinthians and himself in that day (2 Cor. 1:14). John expected to recognize his converts at the Lord's coming. He wrote, "And now, little children, [you] abide in Him, that when He appears, we [the apostles] may have confidence and not be ashamed before Him at His coming" (1 John 2:28). Yes, we shall know as we are known.

Next we learn that God the Judge of all will be there—no longer with the stern frown of justice but with the loving smile of a father. This, of course raises an interesting question, "Will we actually see God, the Father?" On the one hand, we have verses that say that it will not be possible. God is spirit (John 4:24) and therefore invisible. No one can see Him and live (Ex. 33:20). He dwells "in unapproachable light, whom no man has seen or can see" (1 Tim. 6:16).

Yet while people in the Old Testament did not see God in His unveiled glory, they did see appearances of Him. Moses and the nobles of the children of Israel "saw the God of Israel" and were not destroyed (Ex. 24:10-11). When Moses asked to see the glory of God, he was allowed to see His back but not His face (Ex. 33:18,23). When the law was given on Mount Sinai, the Lord showed "His glory and greatness from the midst of the fire" (Deut. 5:24). Isaiah saw the King, the Lord of hosts (Isa. 6:5). But again we emphasize that these were lesser degrees of the divine glory, and not the full revelation.

Now add to the subject the fact that Job had the confidence that he would see God (Job 19:26). And the Savior promised that the pure in heart will see God (Matt. 5:8).

Still another consideration must be added to the equation. The Lord Jesus said, "He who has seen me has seen the Father" (John 14:9). The apostle John said, "No one has seen God at any time. The only begotten Son, who is in the bosom of the Father, He has declared Him" (John 1:18). This means that the Lord Jesus has fully revealed the Father to us. If we want to know what the Father is like, all we have to do is to look at the Savior. So when we get to heaven and see the Son, we will have seen the Father. That may explain how Job will see God and how the pure in heart will see Him.

An incident at a summer camp has taught me not to be too dogmatic on this subject. At a question and answer session, a junior high student asked, "Will we see God when we get to heaven?" With great aplomb, I went through the theological pros and cons listed above. But he was not satisfied. He wanted a Yes or No answer. Again I resorted to the involved reasonings I have just discussed. Again he was obviously dissatisfied; for the third time he asked the same question. Finally I said, "Look, with the eyes we have now, we will not see God because God is spirit and spirit is invisible." Then he triumphantly said, "Well, maybe when we get to heaven, we'll have bigger eyes." That was the end of all discussion. The matter was closed.

Now to get back to other residents in heaven. The Old Testament saints will be there, "the spirits of just men made perfect." Their spirits were made perfect when they believed the Lord; now their bodies are made perfect as well. We will sit at table with Abraham, Isaac, and Jacob as well as with Joseph, Moses, Elijah, and David. It will be the time to get a lot of our questions answered, and to get fresh insights into the sacred Scriptures. But how can we recognize people we have never met before? No problem! In the same way that Peter, James, and John recognized Moses and Elijah on the Mount of Transfiguration (Matt. 17:1-5).

All the redeemed of all ages will be there, singing the praises of the One who loves us and loosed us from our sins by His own blood.

It will be glorious to see our loved ones again, all those who died in faith. Our parting at the river was sad, but the reunion will more than make up for it all.

O then what raptured greetings
On Canaan's happy shore,
What knitting severed friendships up,
Where partings are no more.
Then eyes with joy shall sparkle
That brimmed with tears of late;
Orphans no longer fatherless,
Nor widows desolate.

– Henry Alford

As we fellowship together in Immanuel's land, we will know one another under better circumstances than we have ever known down here.

Hopefully there will be a welcoming committee, made up of those who were won to Christ through our devoted service and faithful stewardship. What a joy it will be to hear some saying, "It was you who invited me here."

And when in the mansions above
The saints all around me appear,
I want to hear somebody saying,
"It was you who invited me here."

– Anonymous

6

No Admission

This is a sad chapter. It is a list of those who will be forever excluded from the courts of heaven. Anyone who fails to qualify can find the reason in one or more of the following categories. The list is complete (Rev. 21:8). People think they have to wait until they die to find out. Not so. The reason is here.

First of all are the *cowardly*. These are the ones who listened to their fears and hesitations and refused to confess Jesus Christ as Lord and Savior. They were more concerned with what their relatives thought about them than what God thought about them. They were afraid of how their mother and father might react if they announced that they had become Christians. They loved the praise of their friends rather than the praise of God (see John 12:43). Notice that they are listed with outrageous sinners, guilty of extremely wicked behavior.

Then there are the *unbelieving*. They may have been moral, upright neighbors, but they refused to repent and believe in the Savior. Perhaps they depended on their good works and sparkling personality to get them through the pearly gates. But they did not accept Jesus as their Substitute, believing that He died to pay the penalty of their sins. They comforted themselves with the vain hope that a God of love would not turn them away. So they did not accept God's only way of salvation.

The *abominable* are sinners who engaged in practices that were disgusting, degraded, and despicable in the sight of God. Idolatry with its accompanying immorality is an abomination (Matt. 24:15). So is the love of money (Luke 16:14-15). Six things that are an abomination to the Lord are "a proud look, a lying tongue, hands that shed innocent blood, a heart that devises wicked plans, feet that are swift in running to evil, and one who sows discord among brothers" (Prov. 6:16-19).

Next on the list are *murderers*, those who violate the sixth commandment. Jesus broadened the meaning of murder from homicide to include anger at one's brother (Matt. 5:21-22). The apostle John added hatred: "Whoever hates his brother is a murderer, and you know that no murderer has eternal life abiding in Him" (1 John 3:15).

Add to the list the *sexually immoral*. This is a broad description that covers fornicators, adulterers, homosexuals, lesbians, in short, all who practice sex outside of marriage. Conventional wisdom says that these behaviors are forms of sickness. God says they are sin. These days it is not politically correct to condemn them, but God says that they will keep a person out of heaven and consign him or her to the lake of fire.

There are the *sorcerers*. This covers people who engage in occult practices: fortune-telling, seances, communicating with the spirits of the dead, and horoscopes (reading the signs of the zodiac). It refers to all forms of astrology, numerology, and witchcraft. Sorcerers use such things as crystal balls, tarot cards, and the ouija board as their stock in trade. God's Word is clear:

> There shall not be found among you anyone who makes his son or his daughter pass through the fire, or one who practices witch-craft, or a soothsayer, or one who interprets omens, or a sorcerer, or one who conjures spells, or a medium, or a spiritist, or one who calls up the dead (Deut. 18:10-11).

Seventh on the list are *idolaters.* At first we think of those who worship graven images or icons. There is a link between idolatry and demonism. The apostle Paul says that when people offer sacrifices to idols, they are offering them to demons (1 Cor. 10:19-20). But in a wider sense an idol is anyone or anything that takes the place of the Lord on the throne of a person's heart.

We come now on the list to *liars.* These are com-pulsive deceivers; they practice lies as a way of life. As a result they find their names on the register of the damned. People may think lightly of lies but God doesn't.

In Revelation 22:15 John gives another list of those who are outside, that is, excluded from heaven. Here he omits the *cowardly, unbelieving*, and *abominable*, and adds the word *dogs.* This title is used for male prostitutes in Deuteronomy 23:18. Since dogs were unclean under the law of Moses, the word is used to refer to the uncleanness of the lives of these men.

Does this mean that people who are guilty of these sins cannot be saved at the present time? Certainly not. If they bow their knee at the name of Jesus, and make their robes white in the blood of the Lamb, they are fitted for heaven. But if they die without repenting and believing on the Son of God, they choose to spend eternity with the Neros, the Hitlers, and the Stalins.

7

The Central Wonder

If the central attraction of heaven is that *the Savior* is there, the central wonder will be that we, the redeemed, are there too. Ungodly sinners all, unworthy of the least of His mercies, gathered from every tribe, nation, people, and tongue, we will be there as everlasting trophies of the marvelous grace of God. Believers of all the ages, cleansed by the blood of the Lamb, will be robed in white garments of salvation. An old chorus says it well:

> *Wonderful Savior, wonderful Friend,*
> *Wonderful life that never shall end,*
> *Wonderful place He's gone to prepare,*
> *Wonder of wonders, I shall be there!*

We will be there in glorified bodies, just like the Savior's resurrected body. There will be no wrinkles, warts, birthmarks, or any such thing. A. T. Pierson comments: "Think of it—when the omniscient eye looks upon us at last, He will not find anything that to His immaculate holiness

35

can be so much as a pimple or a mole on a human face. How incredible!"

F. W. Grant notes: "No sign of old age, no defect, nothing will suit Him then but the bloom and eternity of an eternal youth, the freshness of affections which will never tire, which can know no decay. The Church will be holy and blameless then."

One of the ultimate goals for which God has prepared us is the glorified body, when mortality will be swallowed up by life (2 Cor. 5:4-5). This will take place at the rapture when the bodies of all who have died in Christ will be raised. It is one phase of the resurrection of the just.

That word *resurrection* always refers to the body, never to the soul and spirit. The same body that is laid to rest in the grave will be raised, but it will be raised in a different form. This can be illustrated by a seed and the plant that grows from it. A vital connection exists between them but they are different. There is linkage without likeness. A seed may be drab and unpromising, yet the flower that grows out of it may exceed the glory of Solomon.

So our bodies are sown in corruption. They are perishing, decaying, and returning to dust. Unless they are embalmed, they must be buried fairly soon. But they will be raised in incorruption, forever free from deterioration or dissolution.

Our bodies are sown in dishonor. The mortician may use cosmetics to brighten the face of death, but the fact remains that a corpse is neither attractive or admirable. In contrast, the resurrection body will glow with splendor.

Nothing could be weaker than a lifeless body. It is powerless for any activity. But in resurrection that body will be capable of mental and physical feats that are unthinkable at present.

We are sown a natural body but raised a spiritual body. The natural body with its limitations is suited to life in our natural environment. The spiritual body, though tangible, is suitable to life in heaven as well as on earth. How do we know this?

Because the Lord Jesus lived on earth in His spiritual body after His resurrection, and He is now living in heaven in that same body.

Our present bodies are mortal, that is, subject to death. We will be raised in immortality without the possibility of ever dying.

What else do we know about our resurrection body? We know that it will be like the glorified body of the Lord Jesus. "Christ . . . will transform our lowly body that it may be conformed to His glorious body. . . ." (Phil. 3:21). Our body will glow with splendor. "The sufferings of this present time are not worthy to be compared with the glory which shall be revealed in us" (Rom. 8:18). Paul describes it as "a far more exceeding and eternal weight of glory" (2 Cor. 4:17).

In another place Paul writes: "As was the man of dust, so also are those who are made of dust; and as is the heavenly Man, so also are those who are heavenly. And as we have borne the image of the man of dust, we shall also bear the image of the heavenly Man" (1 Cor. 15:48-49).

In 1 John 3:2 we read: "Beloved, now we are children of God; and it has not yet been revealed what we shall be, but we know that when He is revealed, we shall be like Him, for we shall see Him as He is." One sight of the Savior will transform us into His image. Although each of us will have separate physical identities, we will be like Him in spiritual, moral, and physical perfection. We will, however, never share the unique, incommunicable attributes of God, such as omnipotence, omniscience, and omnipresence.

I am reminded of what Andrew Bonar wrote on one occasion. He had sent Spurgeon a copy of his recently published book on Leviticus. Spurgeon was so pleased that he sent the book back with this note. "Dr. Bonar, please autograph the book for me and enclose a picture of yourself." Bonar did as asked, and added this note: "Dear Spurgeon, Here is the book with my autograph and photograph. If you had been willing to wait a short season, you could have had a better likeness, for I shall be like Him. I shall see Him as He is."

The resurrection body will be a body of flesh and bones but not flesh and blood because "flesh and blood cannot inherit the kingdom of God" (1 Cor. 15:50). We will know as we are known, that is, we will recognize one another: "Now I know in part, but then I shall know even as I am known" (1 Cor. 13:12). We will not be limited by time, space, or matter; we will be able to move effortlessly from place to place, and will appear and disappear at will. Someone has suggested that while we have five senses now, we may have fifty then.

We will have minds that are no longer skewed by sin. Robert Davis rejoiced in this when he realized that he was slipping into the ravages of Alzheimer's disease. He wrote:

> Certainly, one of the first things we will receive is a new mind. How I long for that! As my mind becomes more confused and forgetful, I long for it to become clear. As I can no longer read and accurately remember, I become so frustrated. As my IQ constantly drops, I find myself in humiliating circumstances. I yearn to have my old mental pictures and my old memories return. Learning was always such a joy, and I would love to be able to explore new mental paths.[3]

We will be holy at last. Don't you long for the time when you will never sin again? Never again will we grieve the heart of Christ by our proneness to wander. There will be no boasting in heaven; no one of us will crow that we have reached the gates of pearl by our own efforts or character. Nor will there be jealousy, backbiting, or gossip. Lust will never plague us again. All the works of the flesh will give way to the fruit of the Spirit: love, joy, peace, longsuffering, kindness, goodness, faithfulness, gentleness and self-control (Gal. 5:19-23). The Lord will present us "faultless before the presence of His glory with exceeding joy" (Jude 24).

Sorrow and sighing, tears and crying, will be unknown, whether the anguish of losing a loved one, the grief of wayward, rebellious children, or the heartbreak of a shattered marriage. Twice the Spirit of God reminds us that "God will wipe away all tears from their eyes" (Rev. 7:17; 21:4).

> *God shall wipe away all tears*
> *Some bright glorious morning*
> *When the journey's ended*
> *And the course is run.*
> *No more crying, pain, or death*
> *In that home of gladness*
> *Trials cease, all is peace*
> *When we see His face.*

— Norman Clayton

Life will be free from tension, frenzy, and agitation. Nervous breakdowns and psychological problems will be forever past. No need of Prozac.

There will be no germs or viruses to affect our glorified bodies. Neither cancers nor coronaries will plague us there. Heaven has no need of medicine cabinets, X-rays, or life-support systems. If there were hospitals, every bed would be unoccupied, and doctors and nurses jobless. Never again will a spouse have to watch his or her loved one sink into the oblivion of Alzheimer's disease.

" . . . and there shall be no more pain, for the former things have passed away" (Rev. 21:4). Can you imagine what it will be like to have bodies that are totally pain-resistant? No one will experience the suffering of arthritis, kidney stones, or root canals.

The redeemed hosts of heaven will neither hunger nor thirst "for the Lord who is in the midst of the throne will shepherd them and lead them to living fountains of water" (Rev. 7:17). That promise holds a special, joyful anticipation for persons who have lived with starvation and scarcity of water in this life. But it also applies to those who have hungered and thirsted for holiness, righteousness, and the Savior's return.

In heaven the sun will not strike anyone nor will people be oppressed by heat. If we take this literally, it means that there will be neither sunstroke nor heat prostration. But it could also mean freedom from the heat of temptation and the fires of persecution.

At God's right hand we will enjoy what we were never able to find here on earth, fullness of joy and pleasures forevermore (Psa. 16:11).

"The last enemy that shall be destroyed is death" (1 Cor. 15:26). And what an enemy it has been! Think of broken-hearted parents standing at the grave of darling children. Or the multitudes plunged into sadness by disasters such as the sinking of the Titanic, bombings, random drive-by shootings. Remember the wars that have decimated populations. Atrocities like the Holocaust. How apt are the words of Scripture, "death has reigned" (Rom. 5:14.17). But that reign will be abruptly and finally terminated, and in heaven we will enjoy life that is everlasting.

To have us with Him in glory and in glorified bodies will be the culmination of God's plan of the ages. He will be satisfied (Psa. 116:15). As the Savior looks on us with those kindly, beaming eyes, He will rejoice and we will rejoice. He will see the labor of His soul, and will be satisfied (Isa. 53:11). And we will be satisfied when we see His face in righteousness and awake with His likeness (Psa. 17:15).

> *He and I in that bright glory*
> *One deep joy shall share;*
> *Mine, to be forever with Him,*
> *His, that I am there.*

> — Frances Bevan

8

HEAVEN A PLACE OF PROGRESS

Too often people have imagined heaven to be a place not only of rest but of inactivity, something like a never-ending vacation. A young professing Christian man said, "I think heaven's going to be boring–just lying around all day on a cloud, strumming a harp." Who would want to go to any place so bland and boring? Who would want to be an eternal "couch potato"?

The truth is that heaven is a place of endless progress, growth, and revelation. We can know this from Paul's words in Ephesians 2:7: "That in the ages to come He might show the exceeding riches of His grace in His kindness toward us in Christ Jesus." This means that throughout eternity God will be teaching us what it meant for Him to send His Son to die for us at Calvary. If *He* is going to be *teaching*, then we will obviously be *learning*. Yes, heaven will be a school with God as Teacher and all the redeemed as students. The term length will be eternity. With the Bible as the textbook, the ransomed throng will be enrolled in the course, "God's Grace and Kindness." The subject is inexhaustible.

I personally expect that there will be other subjects. The Bible itself, being an infinite and eternal book, will form the basis of endless study. We have not even scratched the surface in this life. There are treasures in the Scriptures that will thrill our souls on the other side. Mysteries that are now insoluble will be clarified.

It is possible that when we get to heaven, we will see the whole panorama of biblical history unfold before our eyes. Would you like to see what happened when God spoke the worlds into being? I would. Or what the Garden of Eden was like before it was ruined by sin? Perhaps you will see Noah's ship floating serenely above the highest mountains. How would you like to witness the heart-wrenching scene on Mount Moriah when Abraham took Isaac there to offer him as a burnt offering to God? Look! There are the children of Israel crossing the Red Sea with Pharaoh's troops in hot pursuit. And the giving of the law with terrifying lightning at Mount Sinai. Now you see the people of Judah in captivity in Babylon.

Then we come to the New Testament. Bethlehem with the "No Vacancy" sign on the inn. The Lord Jesus giving the Sermon on the Mount. Gethsemane appears with indescribable pathos. Most moving of all, how would you like to see Calvary as it actually happened, and the Lord Jesus suspended on the cross of wood, bearing the sins of the world? Then the resurrection morning and the risen Christ appearing first to the women and then to the others. At present we have our own mental pictures of what happened on those occasions, but none of our pictures agree. Then we will see the authentic versions.

Think of it this way. The light rays that clothed these events are somewhere in the universe. True, they have been scrambled and distorted beyond recognition by now. But if God can retrieve and re-form the bodies of those who have died in faith, would it be impossible for Him to reassemble the light rays of events from Genesis to Revelation so that we could see them? Of course He could. But He wouldn't have to. He could just push the "Play" button and the panorama would unfold before our eyes.

When we watch a parade from ground level, we see only those bands and floats that pass before us. But if we could get up into a high enough building, we could see the whole parade–from start to finish. In heaven we will be at a height that is sufficient to reveal the whole parade from creation to the new heavens and the new earth.

Or consider this. Light rays travel at 186,281 miles per second. The pictorial record of what is happening on earth today will take about 1,660 light years to reach Orion. Another way of saying it is that if we look at Orion tonight, what we see is history, not a current happening. Actually, if we could stand on Orion and look back on earth with a powerful enough telescope, we could see Alexander the Great in his prime (338-328 BC). Or if we could stand on a planet that is between 2,000 and 2,100 light years away, we could see the life and times of the Lord Jesus.

Or think of it this way. Time, as we know it, will no longer exist in heaven. Our calendar is based on the fact that the earth orbits the sun in 365 days, 5 hours, and 48-plus minutes. That relationship will no longer be operative in heaven. Perhaps there will be no past or future, just an everlasting present. If that is so, it means that Calvary (as well as all other biblical events) will be an ever-present reality.

If this seems too complicated, just be thrilled by the fact that the Bible which you have known as black print on white pages will possibly be seen in living color when we reach heaven.

Miracles of Creation

In heaven's school, it seems only reasonable that the Lord will teach us the wonders of His natural creation. At present we have only inklings–example, the dimensions of the stellar universe for example. Who can doubt that "in resurrection bodies, unfettered by gravity, the redeemed of the Lord will have an eternity of time to explore the infinitude of space . . . man will finally reach the stars?"[4]

We will worship the Lord for the marvels of the human body: voice, sight, hearing, touch, taste, smell. For the heart and the circulatory system. For the skeletal structure, the muscles, the nervous system, For the phenomenal achievements of the human brain. We will get answers to our questions about the mind, the soul, and the spirit. We have taken these things for granted far too long.

As we look down from heaven, we will learn how perfectly the old earth was suited to human life: the presence of water, just the right atmosphere, the finely tuned rotation of the earth that produces the seasons of the year.

We will have a new appreciation of God's provision of food for all His creatures–what a feat of logistics! We will see how little we knew about the formation of a baby in the womb.

And we will be amazed that rational people could have ever believed that it all took place by evolution, that behind all the intricate design there was no Designer.

Divine Providence

We will at last be able to look behind the scenes and see how God was working all things together for good to those who loved Him. We will understand His timing and sequence of moves that at the time seemed random. It will be clear then that nothing happened by chance, that there were no accidents, and that what seemed like coincidence was actually divine providence. *Dis*appointments were *His* appointments. All was right that seemed wrong.

In heaven we will see how we were protected by God's invisible army. We will be like the young man in Elisha's day; when the Lord opened his eyes, he saw the mountain full of horses and chariots (2 Kings 6:17). It will be clear that those who were with us were more numerous than Satan's hosts arrayed against us.

It will be an unveiling of how God guided His people, how He harnessed storms to serve His purposes, how He provided the necessities of life, how He made the wrath of men to praise Him. We will see how "the dark threads were as needful in the Weaver's skillful hands as the threads of gold and silver in the pattern He had planned."

And at last, the final solution to the mystery of suffering.

Not now, but in the coming years–
It may be in the better land–
We'll read the meaning of our tears,
And there, some time, we'll understand.

We'll catch the broken threads again,
And finish what we here began;
Heaven will the mysteries explain,
And then, ah then, we'll understand

We'll know why clouds instead of sun
Were over many a cherished plan;
Why song has ceased when scarce begun;
'Tis there some time, we'll understand.

Why what we long for most of all,
Eludes so oft our eager hand;
Why hopes are crushed and castles fall,
Up there, some time, we'll understand.

God knows the way, He holds the key,
He guides us with unerring hand;
Some time with tearless eye we'll see;
Yes, there, up there, we'll understand.

– Maxwell N. Cornelius

Testimony Time

Then, too, there will be the wonders of God in redemption. We will hear the fascinating testimonies of all who have been saved by God's wonderful grace. Each will have one thing in common: they were all saved by grace through faith in the Lord. But each one will be different as to the steps by which he or she was brought in. "Some through the waters, some through the flood, some through the fire, but all through the blood."

Atheists and agnostics will tell how they never had peace until they found it in Christ. Critics will rehearse how they set out to disprove the Bible and ended up as its staunchest defenders. We will hear of how lives of drunkenness and debauchery were transformed into lives of holiness.

The great Christian martyrs will be there together with the Reformers, redeemed by the precious blood of Christ. Buddhists, Hindus, and Muslims will trace the marvelous circumstances by which they heard the gospel and responded.

Not many of the world's wise, mighty, and noble will be there, but multitudes of common folks who heard the Word gladly. Catholics and Protestants, clergy and laity, communists and capitalists will testify how they experienced conviction of sins and turned to the Savior for forgiveness.

There will be testimonies of childhood conversions and of older folks who were saved on their deathbed. One person will tell how he believed the first time he heard the gospel, others after years of running from God.

> *All these were once sinners,*
> *Defiled in His sight.*
> *Now arrayed in pure garments*
> *In praise they unite.*
>   – A. T. Pierson

Heaven will resound with testimonies of the convicting, converting grace of God.

Other Unfolding Revelations

We will see more fully the close link between the material and the spiritual. During His earthly ministry, the Lord Jesus constantly drew spiritual lessons from the natural realm.

> *He talked of grass and wind and rain,*
> *Of fig trees and fair weather,*
> *And made it His delight to bring*
> *Heaven and earth together.*
>
> *He spoke of lilies, vines, and corn,*
> *The sparrow and the raven,*
> *And words so natural, yet so wise*
> *Were on men's hearts engraven.*
>
> *Of yeast with bread, and flax, and cloth,*
> *Of eggs, of fish, and candles,*
> *See how the whole familiar world*
> *He most divinely handles!*
>
> –T. T. Lynch

On earth we had a fleeting glimpse. In heaven we will realize that everything preached a spiritual lesson if we had only had ears to hear it.

Is it possible that when we get to heaven, we will learn that God had other programs going on in places other than the earth? Don't misunderstand me. Earth is the only planet on which there is life as we now know it. Earth is the only place where God planned the redemption of humankind. Only on earth was the Cross erected. In that sense, our planet is unique. But a God as great as ours could very well have programs in other spheres. We find vague references to principalities and powers, rulers in the spirit realm. Nothing in the Bible forbids the idea of divine plans being worked out in inter-galactic space. Those plans, of course, would have nothing to do with our salvation.

Scientist Henry Morris writes:

The reality behind all these "fearful sights and great signs from heaven" (Luke 21:11) can only be that there really is life in outer space! But these living inhabitants of the heavenly bodies are neither super-men in space ships nor blobs of protoplasm in various stages of evolution. They are, rather, "angels that excel in strength" (Psalm 103::20), "ministering spirits, sent forth for them who shall be heirs of salvation" (Hebrews 1:14), none other than God's holy angels. There exists also in the heavens a vast horde of rebel angels, following "that old serpent, called the Devil, and Satan, which deceiveth the whole world"

(Revelation 12:9).[5]

It will be a glorious time. We will all confess with new understanding, "As for God, His way is perfect." Samuel Medley (1738-1799) put it aptly in his hymn: "With all His saints, we'll join to tell, 'Our Jesus has done all things well.'"

9

The Place Itself

One word describes heaven more than any other, the word *glory*. In fact, that word is sometimes used as a synonym for heaven (Psa. 73:24; Col. 3:4; Heb. 2:10). Human language cannot do justice to its splendor, so God uses objects of magnificence and elegance to convey some faint idea of our homeland. Of course, He has to be careful not to reveal too much, because then we would be so anxious to leave this world that we would not be willing to carry on our daily duties. So we must be satisfied with the assurance that "Eye has not seen, nor ear heard, nor have entered into the heart of man the things which God has prepared for those who love Him" (1 Cor. 2:9).

When we think of glory, we might recall weddings of the rich and famous, coronations of royalty, or the opening exercises of the Olympic Games. However beautiful those events are, there is a glory that excels them all.

Just think . . .
Of stepping on shore,–And finding it heaven;
Of taking hold of a hand,–And finding it God's hand;
Of breathing new air,–And finding it celestial air;
Of feeling invigorated,–And finding it immortality;
Of passing from storm and tempest–To one unbroken calm;
Of waking up,–And finding it glory.
                              —Author unknown.

The Bible chapters that are most often resorted to for an idea of what heaven is like are the last two chapters of Revelation. Actually those verses describe the holy city, New Jerusalem. But we are justified in using most of these chapters as referring to heaven, because what is true of a part (the celestial city) is also true of the whole (all of heaven).[6] The time is eternity, because the first heaven and the first earth have passed away. The city is seen descending out of heaven from God, as a bride adorned for her husband.

We are immediately impressed with the abundance of gold. In one place, John says that the city itself is pure gold, like clear glass (Rev. 21:18). Then he says that the street is pure gold, like transparent glass (21:21b). There are several points of interest here, First, all the gold that has ever been mined on earth would fill only a 58 foot cube. We're talking of only about 115,000 metric tons. It is plentiful in heaven. Second, the gold there is transparent. Our gold is pure when it is 24 carat, but it is not clear. Heaven's definition of gold must be different from ours; its gold must be purer than pure. Third, heaven's values differ from earth's. What humans value as currency and jewelry is like concrete or tarmac in heaven. A jeweler's treasure there takes the place of bricks, wood, and cement.

City walls and gates are usually made for protection. In heaven there is no need for security systems. The gates are never shut. Rather they are designed for beauty. Each of the twelve gates, for instance, is an enormous pearl, with the name of one of the twelve tribes of Israel inscribed on it.

The walls are made of jasper and have twelve foundations, each one named after one of the apostles and decorated with gemstones of varying colors. They have been cut and polished and now they radiantly reflect the light.

This is the only city that has foundations, whose builder and maker is God. It is in marked contrast to the cities of this world, which suffer urban blight and countless other problems.

Flowing down the center of the main street is a river of the pure water of life. On each side are fruit-bearing trees that produce a fresh crop every month.

There is no night there (21:25;22:5). On earth, night is the time when crime and lawlessness flourish. But it is also the time when suffering saints long for the first streaks of dawn. In heaven they are in the land of fadeless day where the light is like a jasper stone, clear as crystal (21:11). It does not emanate from the sun or moon but from the glory of God.

There is no more sea (21:1). No separation of loved ones by miles of water. No terrifying storms, no dreadful tragedies on the deep, no accidental drownings of infants at the beach.

On earth we have been enthralled by the sight of snow-capped mountains, by the splendor of waves crashing on a panorama of white sand, by the beauty of the setting sun. In heaven the Divine Artist will paint with a bigger brush.

The glories of heaven defy human description and surpass human understanding. Streets of gold. Gates of pearl. Gemstones of incomparable beauty. But Spurgeon is right when he says:

The streets of gold will have small attraction for us, and the harps of angels will but slightly enchant us, compared with the King in the midst of the throne. He it is who shall rivet our gaze, absorb our thoughts, enchain our affection, and move all our sacred passions to the highest pitch of endless ardor. We shall see Jesus.

10

Worship and Song

Heaven is a place of worship and song.

Some of our most sacred times on earth have been when we worshiped the Lord in the communion service. The heavens bent low and the presence of the Lord was there. It was as if we were in the vestibule of heaven. Such experiences were a little foretaste of what awaits us when the emblematic bread and wine give way to the Lord Himself.

If the worship of the Lord Jesus is so meaningful now, how much better it will be to praise and adore Him in person. Hymn writer Edward Denny reasoned from the good to the best:

> *O if this glimpse of love is so divinely sweet,*
> *What will it be, O Lord, above,*
> *Thy gladd'ning smile to meet!*
> *To see Thee face to face, Thy perfect likeness wear,*
> *And all thy ways of wondrous grace*
> *Through endless years declare.*

J. G. Deck also exulted in the contrast between worship here and in heaven:

> *If here on earth the thoughts of Jesus' love*
> *Lift our poor hearts this weary world above;*
> *If even here the taste of heavenly springs*
> *So cheers the spirit that the pilgrim sings;*
> *What will the sunshine of His glory prove?*
> *What the unmingled fullness of His love?*
> *What hallelujahs will His presence raise?*
> *What but one loud eternal burst of praise?*

Dr. J. Vernon McGee pointed out that every time we read about heaven in the book of Revelation, saints are either getting down on their faces to worship the Lord or getting up off their faces from worshiping God. He added, "If you don't like to worship God, you won't like heaven, because that is the thing with which we will be occupied in heaven."[7]

The problem is that our present worship is flawed by self-consciousness, mind-wandering, pride, wrong motives, and inadequate thoughts of God. John Newton wrote, "Weak is the effort of our heart, and cold our warmest thought," And then he quickly added, "But when we see Thee as Thou art, we'll praise Thee as we ought."

Richard W. De Haan looks forward to the perfection of worship:

> Our adoration will no longer be imperfect.
> Today, in our most sacred moments, whether
> in private prayer or public worship, our
> minds sometimes wander from God and
> spiritual realities. In that blessed day, we will

be in the immediate presence of God, see the face of Jesus Christ, and our hearts will respond in loving devotion . . . . Through eternal ages our whole being will throb with spiritual joy as we live in the light of God's glory. Loving adoration will flow from our hearts as we gaze upon the face of Jesus Christ, our blessed Savior.[8]

In heaven there will be no stain of sin in our love, praise, and adoration. No distractions or hindrances will limit us. We will have enlarged capacities for worship. The thanksgiving and homage we now feel but cannot express will flow without restriction. Someone has said we will be able to show Jesus a love that would burst our hearts if poured into them now. As a man of Scottish background who finds it hard to show love or to receive it, I hope we will be able to cast our reserve aside and hug the Savior without embarrassment.

The glory land will be a place of incomparable music, with songs directed to God the Father and to the Lord Jesus. Some of the lyrics are given to us in the book of Revelation. They begin by extolling the Savior for loving us, washing us from our sins in His own blood, and making us a kingdom of priests (1:5b-6). They exalt Him as the Creator (4:11), Redeemer (5:9-10), and Author of salvation (7:10). They honor Him for His marvelous works, His justice and truth, His holiness, and His righteous judgments (11:17-18; 15:3-4; 16:5-6).

In a crescendo of praise, the songs ascribe to the Lord a mounting series of glories:

Glory and dominion (1:6b).

Glory and honor and thanks (4:9).

Glory and honor and power (4:11).

Blessing and honor and glory and power (5:13).

Blessing and glory and wisdom, thanksgiving and honor and power and might (7:12).

Power and riches and wisdom, and strength and honor and glory and blessing (5:12).

If we could assemble all the world's greatest musicians and commission them to fill a concert hall with the most melodious and symphonic music imaginable, the performance would be tinny compared to that of the redeemed of the ages. The massed choir consists of ten thousand times ten thousand and thousands of thousands, all singing in perfect harmony. Not a sour note.

Heaven's vault with praise shall ring,
Louder and yet more loud;
Millions of saints His worth shall sing
Each heart in worship bowed.

The tide shall still roll on,
That tide of endless praise;
Till every creature to Thy Throne
Its voice in blessing raise.

– Anonymous

There will be instrumental accompaniment. Harps of God are specifically mentioned (Rev. 14:1-3; 15:2). Trumpets will be there as well. If so, why not all the other instruments that were used in the worship of God in David's time? Our Lord is worthy that everyone and everything possible be used in praising Him.

Perhaps the Lord will indulge me in holding a secret conviction (and hope) that we will have Handel's Messiah in heaven. I know we will have the lyrics because the words are straight from the Word of God that lives and abides forever. So perhaps we will have the musical score as well. It seems to me that the notes are wedded to the words in a skill that shows the finger of God. I would like to hear the heavenly choir singing the "Hallelujah Chorus" while I "bow at His feet and the story repeat and the Lover of sinners adore."

It seems as if eternal days
Are far too short to sound His praise.

— W. Spencer Walter

11

SERVICE

Far from being a place of inactivity and boredom, heaven will be a place of service. "His servants shall serve Him" (Rev. 22:3b). Just as we will have enlarged capacity for worship, so we will have enlarged capacity for service.

All that we do will be prompted by our love for Him. The thought of compensation or reward will never enter our minds. We will serve Him because we love Him. It will provide a satisfying way to express fully the love of our hearts to the One who bought us with His precious blood. It's as simple as that.

Our service will be voluntary. No conscription in heaven. It will be the fulfillment of a sincere desire, not obedience to an order.

We will be able to serve Him without mixed motives, envy of others, competition, interruptions, failures, regrets, clock-watching, mistakes—without the slightest trace of sin.

The Bible does not tell us much about the nature of that service. We will do whatever He desires and whatever we know will please Him. The idea of service is closely linked with worship, praise, and prayer. In Acts 13:1-3, the prophets and teachers at Antioch ministered to the Lord in fasting and prayer. Doubtless the prayer included adoration and thanksgiving.

Our service will never become monotonous. For many persons, work down here has often been humdrum repetition. Think of service that is constantly pleasant and interesting. That's what it will be like.

Service on earth often causes perspiration and fatigue. We know from experience what the Lord meant when He said to Adam, "In the sweat of your face you shall eat bread" (Gen. 3:19). But now the curse on creation is gone. Strange and contradictory as it may sound, our service in heaven will mean perfect rest.

It will be service without cessation, because His servants serve Him day and night (Rev. 7:15). Eternity will be too short for us to do enough for the One who gave His life for us.

His servants will serve Him with a service which is perfect freedom and unalloyed delight. Even now there is no service so fruitful, so glad, as the service of God; but then the priestly ministry will be free from all weariness, all imperfection, all restraint.[9]

–Charles R. Erdman

12

Rewards

Heaven will be a place of rewards given out by the Savior Himself. Over the centuries He has been keeping minute, accurate, and complete records. He will not rest satisfied until everything done for Him will be brought to light. His kindness will repay the kindness of His people.

Judgment Seat of Christ

This recompense will take place at the Judgment Seat of Christ, also called the Judgment Seat of God. (At this point it is traditional practice to explain that the Greek word for judgment seat is bema. But since I have never seen that people are any the wiser for that bit of knowledge, I will skip it.) Usually when we hear the words *judge* or *judgment*, they have an ominous ring. We think of a court room, a black-robed judge (stern, of course), and a guilt-ridden defendant.

But wait. Have we forgotten that the words have another meaning? Why don't we think of judges at the Olympic Games, or at a flower show, or at a county fair? In those venues, it is not a matter of hearing evidence and pronouncing guilt or innocence. No athletes are sentenced to prison. No flowers are declared guilty of death. It is a question of awarding prizes for excellence in meeting predetermined standards. This is what the Judgment Seat of Christ is like.

So when we come to this subject, we must clear our minds of any thought of sin and punishment. The believer's sins—past, present, and future—were judged at Calvary when the Lord Jesus as Substitute paid the price in full. He settled the sin question once for all. Christians will never come into judgment on that score; they have passed from death to life (John 5:24). Because they are in Christ Jesus, they are free from condemnation (Rom. 8:1).

The Judgment Seat of Christ is the time when a believer's life and service will be reviewed and rewarded. The place is heaven. The Judge is Christ. All believers will appear. Paul gives the fullest description of it in 1 Corinthians 3:9-17):

> [9.] For we are God's fellow workers; you are God's field, you are God's building.
> [10.] According to the grace of God which was given to me, as a wise master builder, I have laid the foundation, and another builds on it. But let each one take heed how he builds on it. [11.] For no other foundation can anyone lay than that which is laid, which is Jesus Christ. [12.] Now if anyone builds on this foundation with gold, silver, precious stones, wood, hay, straw, [13.] each one's work will become clear, for the Day will declare it, because it will be revealed by fire; and the fire will test each

one's work, of what sort it is. [14.] If anyone's
work which he has built on it endures, he
will receive a reward. [15.] If anyone's work is
burned, he will suffer loss; but he himself
will be saved, yet so as by fire.

So we see that everything done for God's glory–
Paul calls it gold, silver, precious stones–will be rewarded.
All else will be burned and the worker will suffer loss. But
he himself will be saved. It is a matter of service, not of salvation.

Principles of Judgment

There is nothing secret about the principles which
the Judge will follow in awarding prizes. He has been completely up front with us so that we may know in advance
how to run as winners. Here are some of the considerations
that He will employ:

Faithfulness will be rewarded rather than success
(Matt. 25:21, 23; 1 Cor. 4:2). We cannot always be success-
ful but we can be faithful.

It is not the amount of gift or ability that you or I
have but how we have used it (Matt. 25:15-28; Luke 19:13-
28). We are not all created equal. But the Lord bases His
judgment on how we have used what He has given us.

It is not the kind of service that counts but the spirit
in which it is performed (Col. 3:22-24) We should do it as
to the Lord and not to men. And we should remember that
He does not appreciate a bargaining spirit (Matt. 19:27-30).

The desire is rewarded even when it is impossible to
accomplish it (1 Kings 8:18; 2 Cor. 8:12). David was not

permitted to build the temple but God commended him for having the desire in his heart.

It is not the quantity but the heart-attitude that counts (Matt. 10:42). The widow who cast in only two mites is a perpetual reminder of this (Luke 21:2).

It is not how we evaluate our service but how *the Lord* does (Matt. 25:37-40).

> *Deeds of merit as we thought them,*
> *He will show us were but sin.*
> *Little acts we had forgotten,*
> *He will show us were for Him.*

It is not what others see but what God sees and knows (Matt. 6:1-18). If we do anything for public approval and get it, we have already received our reward, that is, public approval.

Anything done for the Lord's people is reckoned as having been done for Him (Matt. 25:40). This opens vast possibilities for feeding Him, clothing Him, visiting Him, and serving Him as truly as if He were bodily present.

No good thing done for the Lord and for His glory is insignificant; it will all be rewarded (Eph. 6:8). There is no distinction between the secular and the sacred. A maid's or a janitor's menial service, when done for God's glory, is as sacred as spiritual ministry in the assembly.

It follows from this that our social status does not count (Eph. 6:8). An immigrant farm worker, toiling in the field, is not excluded from the best rewards at the Judgment Seat. Prominent Christians have no preference over ordinary ones. The first converts in the Christian era will have no advantage over those living at the time of the rapture.

Finally, the Lord prizes endurance (Luke 22:28). It is not enough to begin well; He wants those who will go on well for Him to the end.

Crowns

The prizes at the Judgment Seat of Christ are often spoken of as crowns. Unlike the crowns and honors of this world, the Lord's are incorruptible.

There is the crown of rejoicing for faithful soul-winning (1 Thess. 2:19).

There is the crown of righteousness for loving His appearing (2 Tim. 4:8). When Paul speaks of loving Christ's appearance, He does not mean just having warm, sentimental thoughts about the rapture. Rather it means living in the light of His coming: watching, waiting, praying, and serving.

There is the crown of life for enduring temptation (James 1:12). We forget this when we slide down the slippery slopes of temptation. There is reward for saying No.

Peter mentions the crown of glory for those who are faithful undershepherds of Christ's sheep (1 Pet. 5:4).

Paul strove for an imperishable crown for exercising self-control in the Christian race (1 Cor. 9:25).

There is a special crown for martyrs, those who have been faithful unto death (Rev. 2:10).

Christians are fairly agreed that the only appropriate use of these crowns will be to lay them adoringly at the feet of the Lord Jesus, who alone is worthy.

Other Awards

Rewards are sometimes linked with administration or rulership. In the parable of the minas (or pounds, KJV), for instance (Luke 19:11-27), one faithful servant was given authority over ten cities, another over five cities. In another place, the Lord said to the disciples, "But you are those who have continued with Me in My trials. And I bestow on you a kingdom, just as My Father bestowed one on Me that you may eat and drink at My table in My kingdom, and sit on thrones judging the twelve tribes of Israel" (Luke 22:28-30). Although this refers primarily to the millennium, it may also have an application to heaven. There, perhaps, Paul's puzzling words to the Corinthians will take on new meaning, "Do you not know that we shall judge angels?" (1 Cor. 6:3).

There are other rewards. The Savior promised that anyone who confesses Him before men, He will confess before the Father in heaven (Matt. 10:32). Just think of the honor of being confessed by the Son of God before the Sovereign of the universe!

Special promises are made to the overcomer, that is, to one who confesses that Jesus Christ is the Son of God (1 John 5:5), who overcomes the world by faith (5:4), and who overcomes the wicked one and his false teachers (2:13-14;4:4). He will eat from the tree of life (Rev. 2:7). He will eat of the hidden manna and will receive a white stone with a new name known only to himself (Rev. 2:17). He will receive power over the nations and be given the morning star (Rev. 2:26-28) and will be clothed in white garments (Rev. 3:5). His name will not be blotted out of the Book of Life, but will be confessed before God the Father and the holy angels (Rev.3:5). He will become a pillar in the temple of God, and have the name of the New Jerusalem inscribed on him (Rev. 3:12). He will sit with Christ on His throne (Rev. 3:21).

If you have difficulty understanding some of these honors, don't worry. They will all become clear when we stand before the Judgment Seat.

Full Cups but Different Sizes

In addition to differing rewards in heaven, there will be differing degrees of enjoyment there. Although it is true that everyone will be happy, it is also true that some will have greater capacity for happiness. Or to put it another way, everyone's cup will be full but some will have bigger cups than others. Paul suggests this in 1 Corinthians 15:41-42: " . . . one star differs from another star in glory. So also is the resurrection of the dead."

This raises the crucial question, "How do we determine our capacity for enjoying the Lord and the glories of our Father's house?" We do it by preparing right now for eternity. Let me suggest some specific ways.

First, what we learn about the Bible now determines the initial investment of knowledge of divine things we take with us. Of course, we will be able to improve on that knowledge when we get home, but we will never be omniscient.

Second, the more practiced we become as worshipers of the Savior here on earth, the more we will be able to appreciate and adore Him when we gather at His feet. He will be a well-known Christ to us.

The depth of our prayer life will help. The answers to prayer we have seen will be evidences of His wisdom, love, and power, and therefore cause for endless thanksgiving.

The extent to which we have laid up treasures in heaven rather than on earth (Matt. 6:19-20) will be a gauge of our coming spiritual estate. Otherwise why would the Lord Jesus emphasize it so strongly?

We lay up treasures in heaven by the souls we bring to Jesus. Spurgeon commented, "One reason some saints will have a greater fullness of heaven than others will be that they did more for heaven than others. By God's grace they were enabled to bring more souls there."

In general our spiritual growth and service at the present time determine the extent of our ability to enjoy our eternal inheritance.

This is illustrated in the stories of two brothers. At an early age Dave turned His life over to the Lord for salvation and for service. He became an avid student of the Word. As he advanced as an electronics engineer, he also found doors opening for preaching and teaching. He and his wife were satisfied with a modest standard of living so that they could give first place to what they considered most important. Their home became a hospitality center, a teaching base, and youth magnet.

Jim was saved two years before his brother. He made astonishing advances as an international sales manager. His family lacked nothing in the way of material comforts and pleasures. But his business consumed him. He was never able to draw a line beyond which he would not allow his career to go.

Both men were saved. Both were sure of heaven through the merits of Christ. But Dave is the one you would go to for fresh insight in the Word. Or help with spiritual problems. He always spoke intelligently and enthusiastically about the Lord Jesus.

You could say that both men enjoyed the Lord, but Dave had a greater capacity for enjoying Him. Both their cups were full, but Dave had a bigger cup. So it will be in heaven.

13

Previews of Heaven

In recent years secular bookstores have done a smashing business selling books that deal with near-death experiences. Betty Eadie wrote *Embraced by the Light.* Raymond Moody's contribution was *The Light Beyond.* Other authors like Elisabeth Kubler-Ross added their insights on the subject.

It is interesting how the word *light* figures prominently in the titles and contents of these books. Readers get the impression that death isn't so bad after all. In fact, it is absolutely glorious. No distinction is made as to anyone's spiritual status, whether the person was a believer or not. Such a question is not relevant in the minds of these authors. What seems to be important is that there is light at the end of the tunnel, no matter who you are.

This, of course, is a counterfeit light. It would fit in well with the evil-one's strategy to lull unsaved people into a false sense of security by assuring them that there is nothing to fear. "Satan himself transforms himself into an angel of light" (2 Cor. 11:14).

We are not ignorant of his devices. He comes to steal, kill, and destroy. People think that all is well, but then they die and wake up in the blackness of darkness forever.

Having said all that, I believe that true believers often do have foretastes of glory before they die. Some see the Savior in His splendor and radiance. Others see glimpses of heaven itself.

Stephen

Such a vision came to Stephen, the first martyr of the Christian church. As the enraged mob was pelting him with stones, "he gazed into heaven and saw the glory of God, and Jesus standing at the right hand of God" (Acts 7:55). That changed everything. The bitterness of death was already past. A few deadly stones didn't matter as long as he could see the glory of God and the Savior standing there, ready to receive him. With perfect poise, Stephen prayed, "Lord Jesus, receive my spirit." Then with perfect forgiveness, he cried, "Lord, do not charge them with this sin."

Moody's Coronation

Just prior to Dwight L. Moody's death, his oldest son heard him say, " Earth is receding, heaven is opening, God is calling." The family quickly gathered around his bed. Moody asked, "Is this death? There is no valley. This is bliss; this is glorious." When his daughter Emmy began to pray for his recovery, he said, "No, no, Emmy. God is calling. This is my coronation day. I have been looking forward to it." After a person has seen heaven, earth has no attraction.

Meeting the King

When Frances Ridley Havergal was dying, she sang a song of victory and heaven. Her face became radiant as if she was gazing on the Lord in glory. One of her relatives said, "We knew she was having an invisible meeting with her King, for her countenance was so glad, as if she had already talked to Him. Then she tried to sing again, but after one sweet, high note, her voice failed. As her brother commended her soul into God's hand, she slipped away."[10]

No Dark Valley

My mother spent six months in the hospital as a result of an accident in surgery. One day as her condition worsened, the nurses or attendants took her down to the X-ray room and left her there for a while. The room was dark and cold. She later told us that as she lay there, the Lord Jesus drew near. It was all very real to her. Any lingering fear was gone. There was no dark valley. She faced death triumphantly.

A Father's Triumph

Veteran missionary Christy Wilson tells of his father's homecall. Here is his account:

"On the last day of his life, we were all with him—my mother, my brother Jack, my sister Nancy, as well as my wife, Betty, and myself. We noticed that he was getting weaker and finding it harder to breathe. So I asked him if he wanted to sit on the edge of the bed. He said he would like to.

"I sat next to him and had my arm around his shoulders. As he sat there, he looked up at the ceiling and prayed, 'Lord Jesus, help me.' His face then became radiant.

"'I see Jesus!' he exclaimed. 'I see the Lord.' None of us saw Christ but he did. He saw the Lord in all His glory, just as Stephen did.

"My father then said, 'Bless the Lord, O my soul; and all that is within me bless His holy name.'

"He was so excited.

"Then, because he was so full of joy and relaxed, we helped him lie down on the bed. All five of us stood around him. He then said, 'O come, O come, Emmanuel!' Even though it was in April, we sang this Christmas carol.

"Then we sang his favorite hymns. Among them was *Amazing Grace.* The last stanza goes:

> *When we've been there ten thousand years,*
> *Bright shining as the sun;*
> *We've no less days to sing His praise*
> *Than when we've first begun.*

"As he lay there, my father pointed to a cushion we had given to our mother. It had the words on it, *Happiness is being a Grandmother.* My father pointed to that and said, 'Real happiness is going to be with Jesus. I'm going to be with Jesus . . . today!' He was so excited because he was about to be with his Lord."

When the members of the family had prayed and had sung the Doxology, the elder Mr. Wilson departed to be with Jesus with a smile on his face.[11]

O Grace!

At one time I had a neighbor in the next apartment who had a very unpleasant disposition. He gave every indication of having been weaned on a dill pickle. Another liability was that he was terminally ill. But in the closing years of his life Jim was saved. Really saved. He was a brand plucked from the burning.

I was overseas when he was taken to the hospital for the last time. When I returned, his wife told me that she was at the bedside on his last day. Suddenly she saw him sit up in the bed, look off as if in the distance, and say "O Marge!" She said it was the most enthusiastic thing she had ever heard him say. Jim had seen the glory of the Lord. Then he slumped back down into the bed and died.

Kamwandi

While on a hunting expedition, an African named Kamwandi had a dream in which he saw a broad road dragging him down as if it were a rushing torrent. It ended in a blazing inferno in which men and women were committing the sins they had committed while they were on earth. In his dream a fellow African warned him to get on a narrow path that led into the forest.

Some time later, he accidentally drove a stake into his leg. The wound would not heal, so he went to the hospital in Kalene for help. When he arrived he saw the missionary lady sitting on a stool and telling the sick people about a narrow road that leads to life and a broad road that leads to destruction. He learned that Christ is the narrow road, and he trusted the Savior for his soul's salvation. As soon as the ulcer had healed sufficiently, he went home to his people to tell them about the Lord Jesus.

But the infection again worsened and he had to return to the hospital. He walked from hut to hut, telling the patients of the Redeemer. Then one day he called the people into his own hut and said, "Listen, I hear them singing! O, what beautiful songs!" and he died with a radiant smile on his face.[12]

The Martyrs of Ecuador

When five young missionaries were speared to death by Waorani (Auca) Indians in Ecuador, there was no indication that they had had a near death experience. But thirty-three years later, Olive (Fleming) Liefeld, the widow of one of the men (Peter Fleming), visited the area where the Indians lived. She and her husband Walter were amazed to learn that two of the Indians who had been present when the men were killed heard singing. Above the trees, they saw a multitude of people with hundreds of bright lights.

Is it not reasonable to believe that this was God's welcoming committee, ushering the missionaries through "the gates of pearly splendor?"[13]

Sometimes or Every Time?

There is no question that genuine Christians sometimes do have a near-death experience. They see the Lord. They see the splendor of heaven. They see the indescribable glory.

The question is, "Does this happen to every child of God before he or she dies?" We might not know it at the time. There may be no expression of joy or delight. There may be no emotional outburst. But could it not happen?

We can be sure that God gives dying grace whenever it is needed. He promised, "My grace is sufficient for you . . ." (2 Cor. 12:9). And in another place "As your days, so shall your strength be" (Deut. 33:25b). We may quake at the thought of dying today, but that is not alarming. We don't have grace at the present time for dying because we don't need it. We can be sure that if we were going to die, we would be given strength to face it with quiet assurance.

Perhaps you've heard the expression, "Martyr grace for martyr days." This means that God gave special grace to the martyrs to witness heroically for the Lord Jesus while enduring terrible torture. We read those stories and think, "I could never do that." Of course not. But if the Lord called on you to be burned at the stake tomorrow, He would give you supernatural strength to face it with poise and peace. It is futile to worry in advance about dying. If the time comes, we can be sure that the Good Shepherd will be with us in the valley of the shadow of death. We will not be alone. And if He is with us, that is all that matters.

14

Food in Heaven?

Will we eat in heaven? Why not? It is certainly possible. The Lord Jesus ate in His resurrected, glorified body. His disciples "gave Him a piece of broiled fish and some honeycomb, and He took it and ate in their presence" (Luke 24:43). Since we will have glorified bodies like His (Phil. 3:21), it is quite possible that we will eat also.

It is not only possible; it is probable. Think of the marriage supper of the Lamb at which all believers will be present. "Blessed are those who are called to the marriage supper of the Lamb" (Rev. 19:9). A supper obviously means food.

Further, the kingdom of heaven is compared to a marriage feast (Matt. 22:1-14) and a great supper (Luke 14:15-24). How appropriate. The kingdom will be characterized by the joy, fellowship, and celebration that are associated with such occasions.

Manna is one of the items on the menu of heaven (Rev. 2:17), and so is fruit (Rev. 22:2).

Jesus said that "many will come from the east and west, and sit down with Abraham, Isaac, and Jacob in the kingdom of heaven" (Matt. 8:11). To sit down with these patriarchs means to converse with them, to have fellowship with them. There is at least a suggestion here that it will be at a table spread with good things to eat.

True, we know almost nothing about the physiology of the glorified body, but it is enough to know that it will be capable of enjoying food and drink without any of the processes that are now the result of sin.

Pagan religions often picture heaven as a place where the animal appetites are satisfied by gorging on food, consuming enormous amounts of wine, and in general engaging in an eternal binge. How different is the holy and restrained way in which the Scriptures handle the subject of our godly behavior in the everlasting kingdom.

15

Marriage in Heaven?

Our Lord made it clear to the Sadducees, the liberals of His day, that in heaven people neither marry nor are given in marriage but are like the angels in this regard (Matt. 22:30). This was in answer to a hypothetical puzzle raised by them to make resurrection seem ridiculous. Seven brothers married the same woman in succession as soon as the present husband died. Question: Whose wife would she be in the resurrection?

The question betrayed ignorance of the Scriptures and of God's power. The Bible teaches the truth of resurrection, and His power guarantees it.

The Lord's answer does not mean that glorified believers are angels. Neither does it mean that they will be genderless. It does not mean that a husband will not recognize his wife. Certainly we will not be less aware in heaven than on earth. But the word of the Lord means that the marriage relationship will not continue in heaven, and there will be no begetting of children.

If the exceedingly tangled marital histories of some Christians with complicated divorces and remarriages are a problem to us when we think of heaven, we can be assured that they are not a problem to God. He has solved far bigger problems than this.

16

The Marriage Supper of the Lamb

It was a Jewish custom in biblical times for a man to go to the house of his prospective bride in order to make a covenant of betrothal. This was similar to engagement but more binding. The covenant included a purchase price paid to the bride's father. Once the price had been paid, the man would return to his own father's house to prepare living accommodations. He might not see his bride for a year.

At the end of that time, he and his wedding party would go to claim his bride and take her to the place he had prepared with loving care. The bride knew he would come but she didn't know the exact time. Finally, back in his father's house, the marriage was consummated. After a week or so, the groom presented his bride to the assembled wedding guests.

It was then that the marriage supper or wedding feast took place with great celebration and festivity.

Christ is the heavenly Bridegroom and the church is His bride. He purchased her with His own blood, literally selling all that He had to win her. Now He is in His Father's house, preparing a dwelling place for her. At a time unknown, He will return to take her to their home in heaven.

In due time He will appear with His bride to the wedding guests, and then will follow the marriage supper of the Lamb. This festive occasion is mentioned in Revelation 19:9: "Blessed are those who are called to the marriage supper of the Lamb."

There is a valid question whether the feast is held in heaven or on earth during the millennium. The parable of the wise and foolish virgins (Matt. 25:1-10) favors the latter view. When the bridegroom (the Lord Jesus) returns, the wedding has already taken place in heaven (Eph. 5:27). The virgins who were ready (saved Israelites) went in with the bridegroom. They did not go in to the wedding, as in the KJV and NKJV. They went in to the wedding feast (v.10, JND, NASB, NIV, RSV). This pictures Christ returning with His bride to set up His kingdom and to celebrate His bride.

Whether the feast takes place in heaven or on earth, the important point is to be sure of attending.

17

Babies in Heaven?

What place do babies who die have in God's great plan of salvation? Well, they are assured of a place in heaven for all eternity. The clearest promise to this effect is found in Matthew 19:14 where Jesus said to His disciples, "Let the little children come to Me, and do not forbid them, for of such is the kingdom of heaven" (see also Mark 10:14; Luke 18:16). That phrase "of such is the kingdom of heaven" is decisive. It leaves no room for argument. It does not require that the babies be believers, that the babies be baptized, or any other condition imposed by man.

A similar proof is found in Matthew 18:3 where the Savior said, "Assuredly, I say to you, unless you are converted and become as little children, you will by no means enter the kingdom of heaven." Notice that He did not say that little children had to become like adults. It is the other way around. Adults have to become like little children.

In the parable of the lost sheep (Matt. 18:10-14), the lesson is: "Even so it is not the will of your Father who is in heaven that one of these little ones should perish." "In heaven their angels always see the face of My Father who is in heaven."

Many grieving parents find comfort in the words of David when his baby son died: "I shall go to him, but he will not return to me" (2 Sam. 12:23). David did not specifically mention heaven, but it is not wrong to read that into his consolation.

When our Lord was speaking of children, He said, "For the Son of Man has come to save that which was lost" (Matt. 18:11). When He was referring to adults, however, He said, "For the Son of Man has come to seek and to save that which was lost" (Luke 19:10). There was a sense in which He had to seek adults that was not true of little children.

But this raises a question. Since babies and little children are sinners by nature and by practice, how can a holy God take them to heaven unless they are born again? The answer is found in the character of God: "Should not the Judge of all the earth do right?" (Gen. 18:25). Although it is true that these little ones are sinners, it is also true that they have not as yet been capable of accepting or rejecting the Savior. In such a case, God can reckon the value of the substitutionary work of Christ to their account, even if they know nothing of Calvary. They are safe through the blood of Jesus.

Still another question arises. At what age does a child become personally responsible to respond to the gospel? In other words, what is the age of responsibility? There is no one specific age for everyone. It varies from individual to individual. Whenever a child has received a bona fide presentation of the gospel, and when he or she is capable of responding to the good news and believing in the Savior, then that child is responsible before God and needs to be converted.

One more question. Will babies remain in infancy in heaven or will there be normal growth? On the one hand, it seems difficult to think of a heaven without babies, when they bring so much joy to us down here. If people age there as they do on earth, then heaven would be an enormous geriatric center. When the disciples met Moses and Elijah on the Mount of Transfiguration, there is no suggestion that they were ancient. Erwin W. Lutzer writes:

> Of this we can be confident. A child in heaven will be complete. Either the child will look as he would have if he were fully grown, or else his mental and physical capacities will be enhanced to give him full status among the redeemed. Heaven is not a place for second-class citizens. All handicaps are removed. Heaven is a place of perfection.[14]

Having said all this, we still have to admit that we don't know all the answers about babies in heaven. The Bible does not give us a detailed explanation. But we can rest assured that God has worked it out in a way that will fascinate, please, and satisfy all His people.

18

Knowledge in Heaven of Things on Earth

Do the saints in heaven know what is happening on earth? If so, how much do they know?

First, we can say with certainty that they do not know everything. Those in their glorified bodies will never share what are called the incommunicable attributes of God, such as omniscience, omnipotence, and omnipresence. When John says we shall be like the Savior (1 John 3:2), he is referring to spiritual and moral likeness. When Paul says we shall know just as we are known (1 Cor 13:12), he reveals that we will recognize each other in heaven. But the question remains: Are any events on earth known to heaven's occupants?

It seems clear that when a sinner is saved, the folks in heaven know it. In the parables of the lost sheep and the lost coin, the Lord Jesus said that there is rejoicing in the presence of the angels of God over one sinner who repents (Luke 15:7,10). This does not limit the rejoicing to the angels themselves. It extends to all those who are in the presence of the angels, which surely includes the redeemed in glory. D. L. Moody comments:

Think of it! By an act of our own, we may cause joy in heaven. The thought seems almost too wonderful to understand. To think that the poorest sinner on earth, by an act of his own, can send a thrill of joy through the hosts of heaven.[15]

It is also probable that when a backslider returns to the Father, heaven erupts with rejoicing. We can deduce this from the parable of the lost son (Luke 15:22-24). Our Lord vividly described the celebration when that earthly father welcomed home his wayward son. If this is true in an earthly sense, how much more true would it be in a heavenly sense. The heavenly Father would do no less. And the festivities would be shared by the heavenly throng.

There is something else that saints in heaven may know, that is, when a believer presents himself as a living sacrifice to God (Rom. 12:1-2). This is the New Testament equivalent of the burnt offering in the Old Testament. That was known as a sweet savor offering. It means that the sweet fragrance of the offering ascended to God. When the Lord Jesus presented Himself to God to be fully consumed on Calvary, Paul described it as "an offering and a sacrifice to God for a sweet-smelling savor" (Eph. 5:2 KJV). Heaven was filled with the fragrant aroma. Why should we doubt that this also happens when a believer yields his life and will to the Lord for whatever He wants to do with it?

That is not the only time when the throne room of heaven is filled with sweet perfume. The Philippians had sent a gift to Paul to meet his temporal needs. In acknowledging it, the apostle described it as "a sweet-smelling aroma, an acceptable sacrifice, well pleasing to God" (Phil.

4:18). I conclude from this that any kindness done in the name of the Lord Jesus is known in heaven by the fragrance it disperses.

Finally, I would suggest that the prayers of the saints are known in heaven. In Revelation 8:3-4, God draws back the curtain and we see an Angel standing at the altar with a golden censer. We believe that this is the Lord Jesus, because He is the only Mediator between God and man. He takes a great deal of incense and offers it with the prayers of all the saints on the altar in front of the throne. "And the smoke of the incense, with the prayers of the saints, ascended before God from the angel's hand" (v. 4). Once again heaven is filled with incense, the fragrance of the person and work of Christ. The whole scene is public. All heaven is suffused with the aroma.

Someone once said that secret sin on earth is open scandal in heaven. Well, it is certainly true that it is known by God the Father, God the Son, and the Holy Spirit. But it scarcely fits the biblical description of heaven to think of anything entering there that would cause sorrow, pain, or defilement. We are safer to confine our answer to five things that happen on earth that are known to the redeemed in heaven: the salvation of a sinner, the recovery of a backslider, the consecration of a saint, any kindness done in the Savior's name, and the prayers of believers.

19

PET ANIMALS IN HEAVEN?

It is not uncommon to hear Christians ask, "Will I have my dog in heaven?" Some might dismiss such a question as foolish or at least trivial, but every serious question deserves a thoughtful reply.

When a person has had a dog for eleven years, and that dog has been affectionate, obedient, loyal, and eager to please, how can the owner help being sad when that "best friend" has been taken away in death? Surely we can forgive the sentimentality that thinks in terms of a doggie heaven. When someone has had a riding horse for twenty-eight years, it is a distressing experience to lose it and quite natural to wish that a horse's heaven might exist.

Perhaps it is encouraging to a horse-lover to read of horses coming out of heaven (Rev. 6:2,4,5,8; 19:11). The five horses referred to might be real horses but commissioned for a specific occasion. Coming out of the atmospheric heavens, they are designed to picture conquest, war, famine, death, and judgment.

It is true that in the King James Version, there are frequent references to *living beasts* in heaven, but the preferred translation is *living creatures*. The text makes it clear that they are persons with intellect, emotions, and will.

Solomon once wrote, "What happens to the sons of men also happens to animals; one thing befalls them: as one dies, so dies the other. Surely they all have one breath; man has no advantage over animals, for all is vanity. All go to one place; all are from the dust and all return to dust. Who knows the spirit of the sons of men, which goes upward, and the spirit of the animal which goes down to the earth (Eccl. 3:19-21). However, those words were human speculation and questioning rather than divine revelation. It is man looking at things *under the sun* (an expression found twenty-nine times in this book). Solomon was saying what we would all think if we did not have a Bible.

A woman once came to H. A. Ironside at the close of a meeting and asked, "Dr. Ironside, will I have my dog in heaven?" Instead of rebuking her, his answer was both kind and true. He replied, "Yes, Madam, {pause} if you want Him."

20

HOME AT LAST

No words can even approach an adequate description of the glories of heaven. No mortal mind can take it in. But God has told us enough about it to make us long for it increasingly. Spurgeon said:

> If you did not long for heaven, surely you might question whether heaven belonged to you. If you have ever tasted of the joys of the saints, as believers do on earth, you will sing with full soul:
>
> *My thirsty spirit faints*
> *To reach the land I love,*
> *The bright inheritance of saints,*
> *Jerusalem above.*

J. Sidlow Baxter gives a tenfold picture of final salvation in the uncountable host of saved sinners, transplanted to heaven as the glorified saints:

"Before the throne"—beatific vision

"White robes"—unsullied holiness

"Palm branches"—finalized victory

"They serve Him"—highest ministry

"He covers them"—unending security

"Hunger no more"—fulfillment for ever

"Sun smites not"—felicity without flaw

"He shepherds them"—serenity in His love

"Living waters"—ageless immortality

"Every tear dried"—joy, perfect, fadeless.[16]

Robert G. Lee called heaven "the most beautiful place the wisdom of God could conceive and the power of God could prepare." He hit the nail on the head when he wrote:

> One day when we go sweeping through those gates of pearl and catch our first vision of the enrapturing beauty all around us, I think we will hunt up John and say, "John, why didn't you tell us it was so beautiful?" And John will say, "I tried to tell you when I wrote the twenty-first and twenty-second chapters of the last book in the Bible after I got my vision, but I couldn't do it."[17]

When our believing relatives and friends are taken home to be with the Lord, it is an inexpressible comfort for us to know that they are in the land of fadeless day, consciously enjoying the presence of the Lord and the glories of heaven. We would not want them to return to this wilderness of sin and sorrow.

For us who are in Christ, what a hope, what a prospect! Soon, very soon, the Savior will come to take us to the Father's house of many mansions. We too will be home at last.

Sweet home of my heart! there is One who dwells in thee
Who once forsook thy glories to die for love of me;
And when His blood had bought me the home I could not win,
Thy gates received the Victor o'er death, and hell, and sin.

Sweet home of my heart! It is this that makes thee dear
And daily wings my footsteps with hope that thou art near.
It is His presence in thee that causes thee to be
No strange and foreign country, but home, true home to me.

Sweet home of my heart! There will come a glorious day
When faith and hope and longing will all have passed away;
When Jesus calls me hence, to be with Him where He is,
And find in Him forever my home of endless bliss.

But what for those who are not believers? If they only knew the glories that could be theirs for eternity, they would never stay away. But God does not take them to heaven against their will. They must come in repentance for their sin and with faith in the Lord Jesus Christ. Dave Hunt was right when he said, "It would be as impossible a contradiction for a Christ-rejecter to be in heaven as it would be for a worm to teach calculus or a lion to appreciate great works of art."[18] A sinner would be miserable and he would make everyone else miserable, if that were possible.

No one's situation is hopeless in this life. As soon as people acknowledge their sin before God and receive the Lord Jesus as their only hope for heaven, they can be as sure of heaven as if they were already there.

APPENDIX

"In Immanuel's Land"

Samuel Rutherford (1600–1661) was a fearless defender of the faith, an honor for which he suffered valiantly. "At the instigation of Charles II, who hated him, Parliament had deposed him from all religious offices, and then summoned him to appear before it on a certain day. But when the summons reached him in St. Andrews, Scotland, Rutherford was on his death-bed, and, on hearing it, he calmly remarked, 'I have a summons before a superior Judge;' and to Parliament he sent the message, 'I have to answer my first summons; and ere your day arrive, I will be where few kings and great folks come.'"

Mrs. Anne Ross Cousin (1824–1906), a Scottish poet, immersed herself in the devotional writings of Samuel Rutherford and wove many of his memorable sayings into a hymn, "The Last Words of Samuel Rutherford." For example, he often referred to "the white stone" and "the new name." As his life was ebbing, he said, "I feed on manna: I have angels' food." "My eyes shall see my Redeemer. I know that He shall stand on earth at the latter day, and I shall be caught up in the clouds to meet Him in the air." "Glory shineth in Immanuel's land." On the threshold of glory, he said, "I shall sleep sound in Christ; and when I awake I shall be satisfied with His likeness. O for arms to embrace Him." Then he cried, "O for a well-tuned harp." We find these phrases and many more in the hymn she composed.

Rutherford would rather have died a martyr's death than to pass away in bed. He said, "I would think it a more glorious way of going home to lay down my life for the cause, at the Cross [a public square] of Edinburgh or St. Andrews; but I submit to my Father's will."

Sometimes the poem quoted here is called "O Christ He is the Fountain" and at other times "Immanuel's Land."

Although Immanuel's land refers to the land of Israel in the Old Testament (Isa. 8:8), it is here used as a poetic name for heaven. The Red Rose of Sharon stands for the Lord Jesus Christ. New Jerusalem and Mount Zion refer to the heavenly city. Anwoth was where Rutherford carried on a fruitful ministry for over nine years; it was located beside the Solway Estuary.

The sands of time are sinking,
The dawn of heaven breaks,
The summer morn I've sighed for–
The fair, sweet morn awakes.
Dark, dark hath been the midnight,
But day-spring is at hand,
And glory–glory dwelleth
In Immanuel's land.

Oh, well it is forever–
Oh, well for evermore!
My nest hung in no forest
Of all this death-doomed shore.
Yea, let the vain world vanish,
As from the ship the strand,
While glory–glory dwelleth
In Immanuel's land.

There the Red Rose of Sharon
Unfolds its heartsome bloom,
And fills the air of heaven
With ravishing perfume.
Oh! to behold its blossom,
While by its fragrance fanned,
Where glory–glory dwelleth
In Immanuel's land.

The King there in His beauty
Without a veil is seen:
It were a well-spent journey,
Though seven deaths lay between.
The Lamb, with His fair army,
Doth on Mount Zion stand,
And glory–glory dwelleth
In Immanuel's land.

Oh, Christ, He is the fountain–
The deep, sweet well of love!
The streams on earth I've tasted,
More deep I'll drink above.
There, to an ocean fullness,
His mercy doth expand,
And glory–glory dwelleth
In Immanuel's land.

E'en Anwoth was not heaven,
E'en preaching was not Christ;
Oft in my sea-beat prison
My Lord and I held tryst;
And aye, my murkiest storm-cloud
Was by a rainbow spanned,
Caught by the glory dwelling
In Immanuel's land.

But that He built a heaven
Of His surpassing love,
A little New Jerusalem,
Like to the one above,–
"Lord, take me o'er the water,"
Had been my loud demand:
"Take me to love's own country,"
Unto Immanuel's land.

But flowers need night's cool darkness,
The moonlight and the dew;
So Christ, from one who loved it
His shining oft withdrew.
And then for cause of absence,
My troubled soul I scanned–
But glory, shadeless shineth
In Immanuel's land.

The little birds of Anwoth–
I used to count them blest;
Now, beside happier altars
I go to build my nest;
O'er these there broods no silence–
No graves around them stand,
For glory, deathless, dwelleth
In Immanuel's land.

Fair Anwoth by the Solway
To me thou still art dear;
E'en from the verge of heaven
I drop for thee a tear.
Oh, if one soul from Anwoth
Meet me at God's right hand,
My heaven will be two heavens
In Immanuel's land.

I've wrestled on toward heaven
'Gainst storm and wind and tide;
Now, like a weary traveler
That leaneth on his guide,
Amid the shades of evening,
While sinks life's lingering sand,
I hail the glory dawning
From Immanuel's land.

Deep waters crossed life's pathway,
The hedge of thorns was sharp;
Now, these all lie behind me–
Oh, for a well-tuned harp!
Oh, to join Hallelujah
With yon triumphant band,
Who sing where glory dwelleth,
In Immanuel's land.

With mercy and with judgment
My web of time He wove;
And aye the dews of sorrow
Were lustred with His love.
I'll bless the hand that guided,
I'll bless the heart that planned,
When throned where glory dwelleth
In Immanuel's land.

Soon shall the cup of glory
Wash down earth's bitterest woes,
Soon shall the desert briar
Break into Eden's rose:
The curse shall turn to blessing–
The name on earth that's banned,
Be graven on the white stone
In Immanuel's land.

Oh! I am my Beloved's.
And my Beloved is mine!
He brings a poor vile sinner
Into His "House of wine."
I stand upon His merit,
I know no other stand,
Not e'en where glory dwelleth
In Immanuel's land.

I shall sleep sound in Jesus,
Filled with His likeness rise,
To live and to adore Him,
To see Him with these eyes.
'Tween me and resurrection
But Paradise doth stand;
Then–then the glory dwelling
In Immanuel's land.

The Bride eyes not her garment,
But her dear Bridegroom's face;
I will not gaze at glory,
But on my King of Grace–
Not at the crown He giveth,
But on His pierced hand:
The Lamb is all the glory
Of Immanuel's land.

I have borne scorn and hatred,
I have borne wrong and shame,
Earth's proud ones have reproached me,
For Christ's thrice blessed name:–
Where God His seal set fairest
They've stamped their foulest brand;
But judgment shines like noonday
In Immanuel's land.

They've summoned me before them,
But there I may not come,–
My Lord says, "Come up hither,"
My Lord says, "Welcome home."
The King of kings, before His throne,
My presence doth command,
Where glory–glory dwelleth
In Immanuel's land.

ENdNOTES

[1] Robert Fowler, *Winning by Losing* (Chicago: Moody Press, 1986), p. 148.

[2] *Words of Peace*, Vol. 36, No. 8, Grand Rapids: Gospel Folio Press, p. 1.

[3] *My Journey into Alzheimer's Disease*, Wheaton, IL.: Tyndale Press, 1989, p.134.

[4] Henry M. Morris, *The Stars of Heaven*, Impact Series, San Diego: Institute for Creation Research, January 1974, p. 4.

[5] Morris, *The Stars of Heaven,* p. 4.

[6] Verse 2 of chapter 22 seems to refer to the millennium because it says that the leaves of the tree of life are for the healing of the nations. Obviously the nations will not need to be healed in heaven. However, it could mean that the leaves are God's provision for preserving the health of the nations. It is similar to the expression "God will wipe away every tear from their eyes" (Rev. 21:4). This may just be a poetic way of saying that there will be no more tears.

[7] J. Vernon McGee, *Thru the Bible*, Vol. 2, Nashville: Thomas Nelson Publishers, 1982, p. 885.

[8] *The Heavenly Home*, Radio Bible Class, Grand Rapids: n.d., p. 31.

[9] Charles R. Erdman, *Revelation*, Philadelphia: The Westminster Press, 1925, p. 162.

[10] M. R. DeHaan and H. G. Bosch, *Our Daily Bread.* Grand Rapids: Zondervan Publishing House, 1959, reading for Dec. 22.

[11] *More to be Desired than Gold,* South Hamilton, Mass: Gordon-Conwell Theological Seminary, 1994, pp. 156-158.

[12] W. Singleton Fisher and Julyan Hoyte, *Ndotolu*, Ikelenge, Zambia: Lunda-Ndembu Publications, 1987, pp. 166-8.

13 Olive Fleming Liefeld, *Unfolding Destinies*, Grand Rapids: Zondervan Publishing House, 1990, pp. 235-6.

14 *One Minute After You Die* (Chicago: Moody Press, 1997), pp. 74-75.

15 *Heaven and How to Get There.* Chicago: Moody Press, n.d., p.53.

16 *Explore the Book*, Grand Rapids: Zondervan Publishing House, 1966, p. 349.

17 *Bread from Bellevue Oven*, Wheaton: Sword of the Lord Publishers, 1947, pp. 70-71.

18 *Whatever Happened to Heaven,* Eugene, OR: Harvest House Publishers, 1988, p. 28.